THE TOFU PRIMER

BOOKS BY THE AUTHOR

The Tofu Cookbook
(with Cathy Bauer)

THE
TOFU
PRIMER

A BEGINNER'S BOOK OF **BEAN CAKE** COOKERY

JUEL ANDERSEN
WITH SIGRID ANDERSEN

Book Design by Juel Andersen and Sigrid Andersen

ISBN 0-916870-33-2

Published by CREATIVE ARTS COMMUNICATIONS
833 Bancroft Way
Berkeley, California 94701

CONTENTS

A MISUNDERSTANDING

Little Dutch Karl
and little French Jeanne
Found they couldn't agree.
For he wanted coffee with
tofu ...
And she said "It goes best
with tea!"

Introducing Tofu

TOFU IS MADE FROM SOYBEANS. IT IS HIGH IN PROTEIN AND LOW IN CALORIES AND HAS NO CHOLE- STEROL AT ALL. IT IS VERY GOOD FOR YOU. IT IS VERY VERSATILE. IT IS VERY INEXPENSIVE; THREE GOOD REASONS TO GET ACQUAINTED.

TOFU LOOKS LIKE A WHITE CURD. THAT IS WHAT IT IS EXACTLY. IT IS MADE FROM SOYMILK IN MUCH THE SAME WAY THAT COTTAGE CHEESE IS MADE FROM COW'S MILK.

TOFU CAN BE BOUGHT IN SUPERMARKETS, GROCERY STORES, NATURAL FOOD STORES AND IN ORIENTAL FOOD STORES IN MOST PARTS OF THE COUNTRY.

THIS BOOK IS A PRIMER OF TOFU. IT IS DESIGNED TO START YOU ON AN ADVENTURE IN THE USE OF COOKING WITH A FOOD THAT IS ENTIRELY NEW IN OUR WESTERN CUISINE, ALTHOUGH CHINESE AND JAPANESE PEOPLE HAVE BEEN EATING IT FOR CENTURIES. TOFU IS THE PRINCIPAL SOURCE OF PROTEIN FOR MOST PEOPLE IN THE ORIENT. DON'T BE TIMID. BECOME A FRIEND OF TOFU AND YOU MAY FIND THAT YOU CANNOT LIVE WITHOUT IT.

TWO KINDS OF TOFU ARE WIDELY AVAILABLE. THE USUAL KIND IS SOFT AND IS JUST CALLED TOFU. THE OTHER KIND IS VERY SOLID AND IS CALLED FIRM TOFU. BOTH KINDS ARE SOLD IN LITTLE PLASTIC TUBS THAT ARE SEALED SO THAT YOU CAN LOOK THROUGH THE TOP. THE FIRM KIND OF TOFU WILL BE IN THREE OR FOUR PIECES AND WILL WEIGH FROM 12 TO 16 OZ. REGULAR TOFU WILL BE IN ONE BLOCK WEIGHING FROM 16 TO 24 OZ.

PRESSING TOFU WILL CHANGE REGULAR TOFU TO FIRM TOFU IN A VERY SHORT TIME, SO IF YOU NEED FIRM TOFU AND CAN ONLY FIND THE REGULAR KIND, PRESS IT YOURSELF.

"HERE WE GO!"

SLICE THE BLOCK INTO CONVENIENT PIECES:

MAKE A PRESSING SANDWICH LIKE THIS:

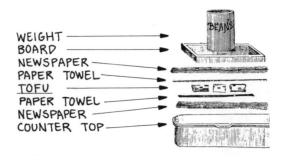

WEIGHT ⟶
BOARD ⟶
NEWSPAPER ⟶
PAPER TOWEL ⟶
TOFU ⟶
PAPER TOWEL ⟶
NEWSPAPER ⟶
COUNTER TOP ⟶

PRESS UNTIL THE TOFU IS AS FIRM AS YOU LIKE.

TWO OTHER KINDS OF TOFU ARE ALSO AVAILABLE – FRESH TOFU AND OLD TOFU. THIS IS BECAUSE MANY GROCERS AND FOOD DISTRIBUTORS DO NOT UNDERSTAND THAT TOFU IS AS PERISHABLE AS COTTAGE CHEESE AND DAIRY PRODUCTS AND MUST BE PROPERLY REFRIGERATED. YOU MAY FIND TOFU IN THE PRODUCE DEPARTMENT NEAR THE BEAN SPROUTS AND WON-TON WRAPPERS, BUT IF YOUR GROCER HAS SAVVY YOU WILL FIND IT IN THE REFRIGERATOR CASE NEAR THE CHEESES AND SOUR CREAM.

BE SURE TO LOOK FOR THE PULL DATE ON THE TOFU PACKAGE. IT WILL TELL YOU WHEN IT WILL BE OLD. IF IT HAS NO DATE IT MAY BE VERY OLD AND YOU WILL DISCOVER THIS AS SOON AS YOU OPEN THE PACKAGE. IT WILL EITHER TASTE SOUR OR SMELL LIKE ROTTEN EGGS OR BOTH.

FRESH TOFU IS SWEET TASTING AND VERY BLAND. IT WILL HAVE A SLIGHT, PLEASANT ODOR AND WILL CERTAINLY NOT TASTE OR SMELL AT ALL UNPLEASANT.

TOFU WILL KEEP FOR UP TO TWO WEEKS DEPENDING ON HOW FRESH IT WAS WHEN YOU BOUGHT IT. TOFU DOES NOT NEED TO BE STORED UNDER WATER, UNLESS YOU CHOOSE TO. THIS ONLY KEEPS IT FROM LOSING THE WATER THAT IS <u>IN</u> IT SO IT WON'T LOSE BULK. STORING TOFU WITHOUT WATER IS A WAY OF GETTING FIRMER TOFU WITHOUT PRESSING IT.✱

COOKING WITH TOFU IS AS EASY AS ABC... THE VARIETY OF USES WILL SURPRISE YOU AND PLEASE YOU. TRY A CREAMY SALAD DRESSING OR A THICK, TASTY SHAKE FOR STARTERS. MAKE A FILLING OR TWO FOR YOUR FAVORITE PASTA OR CREPE OR TORTILLA. RICH DESSERTS ARE A MUST; THEIR SECRET IS HIGH FOOD VALUE AND LOW CALORIE COUNTS.

ORDINARY KITCHEN EQUIPMENT IS ALL YOU NEED FOR TOFU COOKING. A BLENDER OR A FOOD PROCESSOR IS A MUST FOR MANY RECIPES, BUT YOU CAN USE A HAND POWERED BEATER TOO.

NOW, LET'S GO TO IT!

✱ YOU GUESSED IT! FIRM TOFU IS REGULAR TOFU WITH LESS WATER CONTENT.

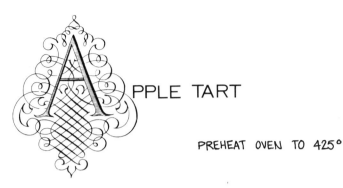

PPLE TART

PREHEAT OVEN TO 425°

CHOOSE 4 MEDIUM APPLES. PEEL, SLICE AND COOK THEM FOR 10 MINUTES WITH 1 TBSP. OF SUGAR AND A DASH OF CINNAMON.

MAKE A COOKIE OR PIE CRUST AND PAT IT INTO A PIE PAN. ARRANGE THE APPLE SLICES IN A NICE PATTERN OVER THE CRUST. SPRINKLE WITH RAISINS OR CHOPPED NUTS, IF YOU LIKE. SAVE THE JUICE FROM THE APPLES.

BLEND THE FOLLOWING INGREDIENTS VERY SMOOTH AND POUR THIS OVER THE APPLES. PLACE IN THE OVEN AND REDUCE TEMPERATURE IMMEDIATELY TO 350°. BAKE FOR 20 MINUTES.

1/2 CUP TOFU
2 TBSP. YOGURT
2 TBSP. SUGAR
JUICE FROM APPLES
1 EGG (OR JUST WHITE)
1 TEASPOON CORNSTARCH
1 TEASPOON VANILLA
1 TEASPOON BRANDY
1/4 CUP MILK
PINCH OF SALT

BLUE CHEESE DRESSING

BLEND ALL THE INGREDIENTS IN A FOOD PROCESSOR OR BLENDER UNTIL VERY SMOOTH AND CREAMY. IF YOU LIKE LUMPS OF CHEESE SAVE SOME OF THE AMOUNT CALLED FOR AND STIR IT IN LATER.

1 CUP TOFU
1/2 CUP YOGURT
1 TBSP. VINEGAR
2 OZ. BLUE CHEESE
   (OR TO TASTE)
GARLIC SALT TO TASTE
1/2 TEASPOON SALT
1/4 TEASPOON PEPPER

P.S. A THICK VERSION OF THIS MAKES AN EXCELLENT DIP!

CURRY SALAD

TO THIS SALAD YOU CAN ADD ANY KIND OF CHOPPED VEGETABLE OR ADD SOME SMALL PIECES OF SHRIMP, FISH OR HAM.

1 CUP TOFU
1/4 CUP MAYONNAISE
1/2 TEASPOON MUSTARD
1/4 TEASPOON SALT
1 TO 2 TEASPOONS CURRY POWDER
1 TEASPOON CHOPPED ONION
LEMON JUICE TO TASTE

MASH THE TOFU WITH A FORK. MIX IN ALL THE OTHER INGREDIENTS AND SERVE ON A HEARTY WHOLE GRAIN BREAD OR ANY WAY YOU WISH.

# DATE-BRAN BREAD

PREHEAT OVEN TO 350°

 CHOP 1 CUP OF DATES AND STIR INTO 1 CUP OF BOILING WATER.

MIX THE DATES AND WATER WELL WITH A ROTARY BEATER OR A FOOD PROCESSOR AND THEN ADD:

1/2 CUP MASHED TOFU
1/4 CUP HONEY
1 TEASPOON VANILLA
1/4 TEASPOON SALT

WHEN THIS IS WELL MIXED ADD THE FOLLOWING DRY INGREDIENTS. STIR THE NUTS IN LAST AND POUR THE BATTER INTO A GREASED BREAD PAN. BAKE FOR ABOUT 1 HOUR OR UNTIL THE CENTER SPRINGS BACK WHEN TOUCHED.

1 CUP FLOUR
1 CUP UNPROCESSED BRAN
2 TEASPOONS BAKING POWDER
1/2 TEASPOON BAKING SODA
1/2 CUP NUTS OR SEEDS

EMPANADAS

PREHEAT OVEN TO 400°

AN EMPANADA IS A SMALL PASTRY TURNOVER FILLED WITH ANYTHING YOU LIKE. MAKE THEM SMALL FOR APPETIZERS OR LARGER FOR LUNCHES, SUPPERS OR PICNICS.

YOU WILL NEED CRUST FOR A DOUBLE CRUST PIE. ROLL TO ABOUT 1/8" THICK AND CUT INTO CIRCLES. FILL ONE HALF AND FOLD THE OTHER SIDE OVER, SEALING THE EDGE WELL WITH A FORK. BAKE ON A COOKIE SHEET FOR ABOUT 10 MINUTES UNTIL NICELY BROWNED. THIS RECIPE WILL MAKE ABOUT 20 APPETIZER SIZE EMPANADAS.

1 CUP MASHED TOFU
1/2 CUP COTTAGE CHEESE
1/4 CUP GRATED CHEESE (ANY KIND)
1/4 TO 1/2 CUP CHOPPED GREEN CHILES
1 TEASPOON CHILE POWDER (TO TASTE)
1/2 TEASPOON SALT
2 TBSP. FLOUR, OR MORE IF FILLING IS VERY WET

FUDGE FROM THE OVEN

PREHEAT OVEN TO 350°

1 TEASPOON VANILLA
1/3 CUP COCOA
2 TBSP. OIL OR MELTED BUTTER
1/2 CUP MASHED TOFU

COMBINE THE ABOVE IN A FOOD PROCESSOR OR A MIXING BOWL AND BEAT WELL. THEN ADD:

1/4 CUP UNPROCESSED BRAN
2/3 CUP SUGAR
1/2 TEASPOON BAKING POWDER
1/4 TEASPOON SALT
1/3 CUP FLOUR

BEAT THIS QUICKLY AND THEN <u>STIR</u> IN 1/2 CUP CHOPPED NUTS. BAKE IN A GREASED 8×10 PAN FOR NO MORE THAN 20 MINUTES. COOL AND CUT INTO SQUARES.

12

GARLIC SAUCE

FOR A DIP OR FOR FISH
OR VEGETABLES

COMBINE IN A BLENDER OR FOOD
PROCESSOR AND BLEND UNTIL VERY SMOOTH. CHILL
FOR SEVERAL HOURS OR OVERNIGHT BEFORE SERVING.

3 GARLIC CLOVES
1 CUP MASHED TOFU
1/4 CUP OLIVE OIL
1/4 CUP VINEGAR
1/4 TEASPOON SALT
PEPPER TO TASTE
WATER TO THIN, IF NECESSARY

Repas à 2 services de 20 à 30 couverts.

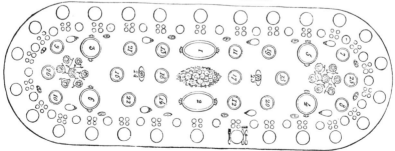

13

AMBURGER…

OR TOFUBURGER WITH HAM

2 CUPS FIRM TOFU, MASHED
1/4 CUP FLOUR
1/2 TO 1 CUP DICED HAM
2 TBSP. OIL
1/4 CUP CHOPPED ONION
1/4 CUP CHOPPED PARSLEY
SALT TO TASTE
PEPPER TO TASTE

MIX ALL INGREDIENTS TOGETHER AND FORM INTO PATTIES. FRY IN HOT OIL OR BAKE IN A 400° OVEN UNTIL GOLDEN BROWN AND CRUSTY.

Autres *Grils* On en fait tous les jours de nouveaux,

Nouveau modèle.

P.S. THE BASIC MIX IS TOFU AND FLOUR. THE FLAVOR CAN BE ALTERED AT WILL!

ITALIAN PARMIGIANA

PREHEAT OVEN TO 350°

FOR THIS RECIPE YOU WILL NEED ABOUT ONE QUART OF ITALIAN SAUCE OF YOUR CHOICE.

12 1/2" SLICES OF VERY FIRM TOFU

2 EGGS
1/2 TEASPOON SALT
1/4 TEASPOON OREGANO
1/4 TEASPOON BASIL LEAVES
PEPPER TO TASTE

1 CUP BREAD CRUMBS

MIX THE EGGS WITH THE FLAVORINGS. DIP THE TOFU SLICES IN THE EGG MIXTURE AND THEN IN BREADCRUMBS UNTIL THEY ARE NICELY COATED. FRY THE SLICES IN OIL UNTIL THEY ARE BROWN ON BOTH SIDES.

ARRANGE THE SLICES IN A BAKING DISH. FILL THE EMPTY SPACES WITH CHOPPED OLIVES AND MUSHROOMS. POUR SAUCE OVER TOFU SLICES AND TOP WITH:
1/4 CUP PARMESAN CHEESE

BAKE COVERED FOR ABOUT 15 MINUTES. REMOVE COVER AND TOP WITH SLICES OF MOZZARELLA OR JACK CHEESE. BAKE UNTIL CHEESE MELTS AND IS BUBBLY.

JAMBALAYA

A CREOLE DISH

12 SLICES FIRM TOFU 1/2" THICK
1/4 CUP OIL, OR MORE FOR FRYING

FRY THE TOFU SLICES UNTIL THEY ARE CRISP AND LIGHTLY BROWNED. DRAIN AND SET ASIDE.

1 LARGE ONION, CHOPPED
1 GREEN PEPPER, DICED
1/2 CUP DICED CELERY
1 LARGE TOMATO, SEEDED
   AND CHOPPED
1 CUP RICE
1 BAY LEAF, BROKEN UP
1/2 TEASPOON THYME
1/2 CUP CHOPPED PARSLEY
1/4 CUP OIL

SAUTÉ RICE, VEGETABLES AND HERBS IN OIL UNTIL RICE IS WHITE. ADD 2 CUPS CHICKEN STOCK OR BOUILLON AND COOK UNTIL RICE IS DONE. ARRANGE TOFU SLICES IN A CASSEROLE AND TOP WITH COOKED RICE. ADD MUSHROOMS AND OLIVES IF YOU LIKE AND FINISH IN THE OVEN FOR JUST A FEW MINUTES.

KAHLUA SHAKE

1 CUP TOFU
1/2 CUP STRONG COFFEE
1 TEASPOON COCOA
1 TBSP. SUGAR
1 TEASPOON VANILLA
PINCH OF SALT
1 OZ. KAHLUA OR TIA MARIA

BLEND UNTIL SMOOTH IN A BLENDER OR FOOD PROCESSOR. ADD MORE COFFEE TO THIN, IF NECESSARY. CHILL AND SERVE.

A Little Girl asked some Kittens to tea,
To eat some tofu from France,
And their Mother came too to enjoy a view,
And afterwards play for the dance.
But the Kittens were rude & grabbed their food,
And treated the Dolls with jeers,
Which caused their Mother an aching heart
And seven or eight large tears.

 EMON CHIFFON PIE

A

YOU WILL NEED 1 PREBAKED PIE SHELL FOR AN 8" OR 9" PIE. THEN COMBINE IN A BLENDER JAR:

B

PEEL FROM 1/2 LEMON
1/4 CUP WATER

CHOP UNTIL THE PEEL IS FINE. THEN ADD:

3/4 CUP TOFU
2 EGG YOLKS (SAVE WHITES)
1/2 CUP SUGAR
1/4 CUP WATER
PINCH OF SALT

C

POUR THIS MIXTURE INTO A HEAVY BOTTOM SAUCEPAN AND HEAT UNTIL IT BEGINS TO SIMMER. <u>DO NOT BOIL.</u> SET ASIDE WHILE YOU MIX:

D

1 TBSP. UNFLAVORED GELATIN SOFTENED IN
1/2 CUP COLD WATER AND
1/3 CUP LEMON JUICE

ADD THIS TO THE HOT MIXTURE AND STIR UNTIL THE GELATIN IS MELTED. BLEND AGAIN AND REFRIGERATE UNTIL SET. WHEN SET, FIRST BEAT THE EGGWHITES UNTIL STIFF. THEN BEAT THE LEMON MIXTURE UNTIL FOAMY. FOLD THE EGGWHITES WITH THE LEMON MIXTURE AND POUR INTO PIE SHELL. REFRIGERATE OVERNIGHT BEFORE SERVING.

 ARINATED TOFU

FIRM TOFU CAN BE MARINATED IN ANY ONE OF YOUR FAVORITE MARINADES. IT CAN BE SLICED OR CUBED OR CUT IN ANY SHAPE. IT CAN BE FRIED OR BAKED OR USED IN CASSEROLES. TRY THIS WAY:

8 SLICES FIRM TOFU CUT 1/2" THICK

COMBINE IN BLENDER:

1/4 CUP SOY SAUCE
1/4 CUP WATER
1 TBSP. HONEY
1 SMALL CLOVE GARLIC
1/4 TEASPOON GINGER
1 TBSP. VINEGAR

BLEND UNTIL SMOOTH. POUR OVER TOFU SLICES AND MARINATE FOR SEVERAL HOURS OR OVERNIGHT. PLACE SLICES ON A GREASED COOKIE SHEET AND BAKE IN A 350° OVEN UNTIL COOKED THE WAY YOU LIKE THEM. THEY WILL GET CHEWIER THE MORE YOU BAKE THEM.

NOODLE CASSEROLE

PREHEAT OVEN TO 350°

COOK 1/2 LB. OF WIDE NOODLES ACCORDING TO DIRECTIONS ON THE PACKAGE. DRAIN THEM AND RINSE WITH COLD WATER. USE HALF THE NOODLES FOR THE BOTTOM LAYER IN A 8 OR 9 INCH CASSEROLE THAT HAS BEEN GREASED AND DUSTED WITH PARMESAN CHEESE. THEN MASH TOGETHER:

1 CUP TOFU
4 MINCED SCALLIONS OR 1/4 CUP CHOPPED ONION
1/2 CUP BREADCRUMBS
2 TBSP. WHEAT GERM
1/4 CUP CHOPPED PARSLEY
1/2 TEASPOON FENNEL SEED
1/2 CUP CHOPPED GREEN OR BLACK OLIVES
1/2 TEASPOON SALT
PEPPER TO TASTE

SPREAD THIS OVER THE NOODLES AND THEN SPREAD OTHER HALF OF THE NOODLES OVER THIS. THEN BEAT:

2 EGGS
1/2 CUP MILK
1/4 CUP PARMESAN CHEESE

POUR THIS OVER THE TOP. DOT WITH BUTTER AND BAKE AT 350° FOR 45 MINUTES.

ONION-POTATO PIE

PREHEAT OVEN TO 450°

PREPARE A PIE CRUST IN A 9 INCH PAN.

1 LARGE ONION CHOPPED
1 LARGE POTATO, DICED OR GRATED
2 TBSP. OIL
1/2 TEASPOON CARAWAY SEED
1 CHOPPED OR GRATED CARROT (OPTIONAL)

SAUTÉ THE ABOVE INGREDIENTS IN OIL UNTIL THE POTATO IS FULLY COOKED. THEN BEAT TOGETHER:

1 CUP MASHED TOFU
2 TBSP. FLOUR
1/2 TEASPOON SALT
1 EGG
1 CUP MILK
PEPPER TO TASTE

SPREAD ONION POTATO MIXTURE OVER PIE CRUST. POUR TOFU MIXTURE OVER THIS. SPRINKLE WITH SOME GRATED CHEESE. PLACE IN OVEN AND REDUCE TEMP. IMMEDIATELY TO 350°. BAKE FOR 20 MINUTES OR UNTIL AN INSERTED KNIFE COMES OUT CLEAN. SERVE AS A MAIN DISH WITH GREENS AND SALAD.

PRUNE WHIP

COOK 1/2 LB. PRUNES IN 2 CUPS OF WATER WITH 1/2 LEMON AND 1/2 CUP SUGAR. PIT THE PRUNES; STRAIN AND SAVE THE PRUNE JUICE.

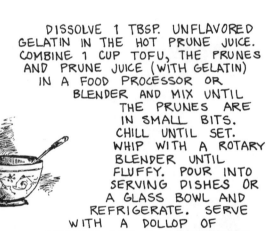

DISSOLVE 1 TBSP. UNFLAVORED GELATIN IN THE HOT PRUNE JUICE. COMBINE 1 CUP TOFU, THE PRUNES AND PRUNE JUICE (WITH GELATIN) IN A FOOD PROCESSOR OR BLENDER AND MIX UNTIL THE PRUNES ARE IN SMALL BITS. CHILL UNTIL SET. WHIP WITH A ROTARY BLENDER UNTIL FLUFFY. POUR INTO SERVING DISHES OR A GLASS BOWL AND REFRIGERATE. SERVE WITH A DOLLOP OF YOGURT AND A TEASPOONFUL OF JAM.

QUICHE LORRAINE

PREHEAT OVEN TO 350°

ONE 9" UNBAKED PIE SHELL

CUT 1/2 LB. BACON INTO 1/2" SQUARES AND FRY CRISP. DRAIN AND SPREAD OVER BOTTOM OF CRUST. THEN COMBINE THE FOLLOWING IN A BLENDER OR FOOD PROCESSOR:

1 CUP TOFU
1 CUP MILK
1 TEASPOON LEMON JUICE
1 TBSP. CORNSTARCH
1 TEASPOON WORCESTERSHIRE
  SAUCE
1/4 CUP GRATED PARMESAN
  OR ROMANO CHEESE
1 EGG
1/2 TEASPOON SALT
PEPPER TO TASTE

BLEND UNTIL VERY SMOOTH; POUR OVER BACON IN THE PIE SHELL. BAKE FOR ABOUT 30 MINUTES UNTIL EDGES BEGIN TO PUFF AND CRACK AND THE CENTER IS FAIRLY SET. COOL FOR 5 MINUTES BEFORE SERVING.

23

# RAISIN-NUT (CHESS) PIE

PREHEAT OVEN TO 350°

ONE UNBAKED 8 OR 9 INCH PIE SHELL

COMBINE IN BLENDER OR FOOD PROCESSOR UNTIL VERY SMOOTH:

1 CUP TOFU
1/3 CUP WATER
2 TBSP. FLOUR
1/2 CUP SUGAR
1 TEASPOON VANILLA
1 TBSP. OIL
1/4 TEASPOON SALT

TO THIS MIXTURE STIR IN 1 CUP OF RAISINS AND 1 CUP OF WALNUTS OR PECANS. POUR THIS INTO THE PIE SHELL AND BAKE FOR 40 MINUTES UNTIL AN INSERTED KNIFE COMES OUT CLEAN. SERVE WARM OR COLD.

 CAMPI

4 SLICES FIRM TOFU
1/4 LB. BUTTER OR MARGARINE
2 CLOVES GARLIC, CHOPPED

CUT THE TOFU INTO 1/2"
CUBES. MELT BUTTER AND ADD GARLIC
AND TOFU CUBES. SAUTÉ FOR A FEW
MINUTES. ADD 1/4 LB. SHRIMP MEAT,
IF DESIRED.

1/2 CUP BREADCRUMBS
1 SCALLION, CHOPPED FINE
2 TBSP. CHOPPED PARSLEY
1 TEASPOON PAPRIKA
SALT AND PEPPER TO TASTE

ARRANGE THE TOFU AND
SHRIMP IN A CASSEROLE. TOP
WITH CRUMBS MIXED WITH
OTHER INGREDIENTS. BROWN
UNDER BROILER FOR A FEW
MINUTES OR BAKE AT 450°
UNTIL BROWNED. SERVE
WITH VEGETABLES, GREEN
SALAD AND CRUSTY
FRENCH BREAD.

TOFU·HOW TO MAKE IT!

YOU CAN MAKE YOUR OWN TOFU. YOU WILL GET GREAT SATISFACTION FROM PROVIDING YOUR OWN PROTEIN. IT IS AS EASY AS MAKING BREAD AND IT IS AS MUCH FUN. YOU WILL USE:

> 1 POUND OF DRY SOYBEANS
> 28-30 CUPS OF WATER (ABOUT 7 1/2 QTS.)
> 3 1/2 TEASPOONS EPSOM SALTS

YOU WILL ALSO NEED TWO SPECIAL UTENSILS:

1. A PRESSING SACK MADE OF A STRONG, FINE MESH, LIKE GAUZE OR CURTAIN MATERIALS.

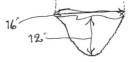

16"
12"

2. A MOLD WITH A CAPACITY OF ABOUT TWO QUARTS WITH A FLAT LID THAT FITS INSIDE. (IMPROVISE WITH ANYTHING THAT WORKS SUCH AS PLASTIC CONTAINERS, COLANDERS, COFFEE CANS, ETC. IT MUST HAVE LOTS OF ° ° ° ° HOLES)

TOFU (CONT.)

BE SURE TO READ THIS
PROCESS THROUGH
BEFORE YOU BEGIN.
(IT HELPS!)

1. WASH THE BEANS AND SOAK THEM OVERNIGHT IN ABOUT 10 CUPS OF WATER.

2. PUT 2 CUPS OF WATER IN A LARGE POT (AT LEAST 12 QUART CAPACITY) AND PLACE OVER <u>MEDIUM</u> HEAT. DRAIN THE BEANS AND GRIND THEM IN A BLENDER USING 1 1/2 CUPS BEANS TO 2 CUPS OF WATER. ADD THIS MASH TO THE COOKING POT AS YOU GO ALONG. <u>KEEP TRACK OF THE WATER YOU USE.</u>

3. BRING THE SOY-WATER MIXTURE TO A BOIL AND COOK FOR 20 TO 30 MINUTES. (THIS GETS RID OF THE "TRYPSIN" WHICH PREVENTS US FROM ASSIMILATING SOY PROTEIN.)

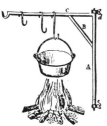

TOFU (CONT.)

4. WHILE THE MASH COOKS WET THE PRESSING SACK AND SPREAD IT OVER A COLANDER WHICH IS PLACED OVER A LARGE BOWL OR POT TO CATCH THE SOY LIQUID. POUR THE COOKED SOY MASH THROUGH THE SACK ADDING COLD WATER TO COOL AND DILUTE THE LIQUID. (THIS LIQUID = SOYMILK) KEEP TRACK OF THE WATER YOU USE. USE ALL BUT 2 CUPS, I.E. 28 CUPS. TWIST AND PRESS THE SACK TO GET AS MUCH SOYMILK AS POSSIBLE.

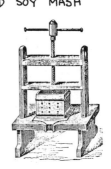

Taille – légumes.

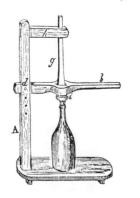

P.S. AT THIS POINT YOU HAVE MADE SOYMILK AND YOU CAN PUT SOME ASIDE IN A BOTTLE AND REFRIGERATE TO USE INSTEAD OF COW'S MILK WHEREVER MILK IS CALLED FOR. SOYMILK IS GOOD FOR PEOPLE ALLERGIC TO COW'S MILK.

TOFU (CONT.)

5. POUR THE SOYMILK BACK IN THE
COOKING POT AND REHEAT IT TO
WHILE IT HEATS MIX THE
AGENT, EPSOM SALTS, WITH THE
2 CUPS OF WATER. WHEN THE
BOILING REMOVE IT FROM THE
STIR IN ABOUT 3/4 CUP OF THE
SALT SOLUTION. WATCH FOR

WASHED
BOILING.
CURDLING
REMAINING
SOYMILK IS
HEAT AND
EPSOM
CURDLING TO BEGIN. ADD ANOTHER 1/4 CUP AND STIR
VERY GENTLY. (TOO MUCH AGITATION MAKES DENSE
TOFU. IT DOESNT HURT IT   AND YOU
MAY PREFER IT THAT WAY.)   LET IT
STAND ABOUT 3 MINUTES.   IF IT
HAS NOT CURDLED ADD MORE
SOLIDIFIER, STIRRING GENTLY   UNTIL
DEFINITE CURDS FORM AND THE   WHEY
BECOMES CLEAR AND YELLOW.

6. LET THE CURDS
AND WHEY STAND WHILE YOU
PREPARE THE MOLD. REMOVE
THE SOLID MASS OF SOY
LEAVINGS FROM THE PRESSING
SACK. THIS IS CALLED OKARA*.
WASH THE SACK AND ARRANGE IT IN THE
MOLD. LADLE THE CURDS INTO THE MOLD,
ALLOWING THE WHEY TO RUN
OFF FREELY.

"WHERE'S THE TOFU, JUD?"

TOFU (CONT.)

6. (CONT.) FOLD THE CLOTH OVER THE CURDS AND WEIGHT THE LID WITH 1 LB. LET IT STAND LIKE THIS FOR 10 TO 20 MINUTES. REMOVE THE WEIGHT AND IMMERSE THE MOLD IN COLD WATER. WHEN COOLED REMOVE THE BAG, UNDER WATER. STORE THE TOFU IN THE REFRIGERATOR, IT WILL KEEP UP TO 2 WEEKS.

* OKARA IS AN EXCELLENT ADDITION TO BREADS AND BAKED GOODS. USE IT AS YOU WOULD BRAN. IT IS HIGH FIBER, LOW CALORIE AND HAS LOTS OF PROTEIN.

Sing, sing! What shall we sing?
The cat's run away with the tofu-bag string

KNIT, DOROTHY, KNIT,
THE SUNBEAMS ROUND THEE FLIT,
SO MERRY THE MINUTES GO BY, GO BY,
WHILE FAST THY FINGERS FLY, THEY FLY,
    KNIT, DOROTHY, KNIT.

SING, DOROTHY, SING,
THE BIRDS ARE ON THE WING,
'T IS BETTER TO SING THAN TO SIGH, TO SIGH,
WHILE FAST THY FINGERS FLY, THEY FLY,
    SING, DOROTHY, SING.

FLY, DOROTHY, FLY,
THE FIRE IS MUCH TOO HIGH,
IF TOFU BURNS YOU MUST THROW IT AWAY,
SO RUN AND SAVE IT, YOU CAN, YOU MAY,
    FLY, DOROTHY, FLY.

UPSIDEDOWN CAKE

PREHEAT OVEN TO 350°

IN A 9 INCH SKILLET MELT 1/4 CUP OF BUTTER. TO THIS ADD 1/4 CUP HONEY OR BROWN SUGAR. STIR UNTIL SWEETENER IS DISSOLVED. ARRANGE ANY KIND OF DRAINED FRUIT AND WHOLE NUTMEATS ON THE SWEET MIXTURE. THEN COMBINE THE FOLLOWING INGREDIENTS IN A FOOD PROCESSOR OR MIXER:

1/3 CUP TOFU
3/4 CUP MILK
1 TEASPOON VANILLA
1/4 TEASPOON SALT
1/4 CUP VEGETABLE
    OIL

BEAT UNTIL VERY SMOOTH AND ADD:

1/3 CUP SUGAR
    (GRADUALLY)
2 TEASPOONS BAKING
    POWDER

THEN ADD 2 CUPS FLOUR, A LITTLE AT A TIME WHILE MIXING. POUR THE BATTER OVER THE FRUIT AND SWEET MIXTURE AND BAKE IN A 350° OVEN FOR ABOUT 30 MINUTES OR UNTIL THE CAKE SPRINGS BACK WHEN TOUCHED. TURN UPSIDE DOWN ON A SERVING PLATE WHEN STILL HOT FROM THE OVEN.

VEGETABLE STIR-FRY

FOUR 1/2 INCH SLICES OF FIRM TOFU CUT INTO BITE SIZED PIECES AND DRAINED ON PAPER TOWELS.

1/2 CUP OIL HEATED IN A WOK OR SKILLET.

FRY THE TOFU IN THE HEATED OIL UNTIL BROWN AND CRISP. DRAIN ON PAPER TOWELS AND SET ASIDE. PREPARE VEGETABLES FOR COOKING IN BITE SIZED PIECES AND FRY OR SAUTE THEM IN A SMALL AMOUNT OF OIL. USE ONIONS, SCALLIONS, CARROTS, ZUCCHINI, TOMATOES AND ANYTHING YOU LIKE. START WITH THE VEGETABLES THAT TAKE LONGEST TO COOK, SUCH AS CARROTS AND ONIONS AND ADD THE SHORTER COOKING ONES LATER, SUCH AS ZUCCHINI AND SPROUTS. ADD TOMATOES LAST. WHEN THE

Légumier.

VEGETABLES ARE COOKED TO YOUR LIKING ADD THE FOLLOWING SAUCE :

1/4 CUP SOY SAUCE
1/4 CUP WATER
1/2 TEASPOON GARLIC POWDER
1/2 CUP WINE
1 TBSP. CORNSTARCH

STIR UNTIL THE SAUCE IS THICKENED. ADD THE TOFU AND STIR UNTIL TOFU IS REHEATED. SERVE WITH RICE.

WHOLE GRAIN GRIDDLE CAKES

THESE PANCAKES ARE MADE WITHOUT EGGS AND ARE WHOLESOME AND DELICIOUS. COMBINE THE FOLLOWING IN A FOOD PROCESSOR OR A BLENDER:

1/2 CUP TOFU
1/2 CUP BUTTERMILK
1/4 TEASPOON SALT
1/4 CUP OIL OR MELTED BUTTER

BLEND THIS VERY SMOOTH, THEN ADD:

2 TEASPOONS BAKING POWDER
1/2 TEASPOONS BAKING SODA
1 CUP WHOLE WHEAT FLOUR
1/4 CUP WHEAT GERM
1/4 CUP UNPROCESSED BRAN
2 TBSP. 7 GRAIN CEREAL, OATMEAL OR SOY GRITS

STIR UNTIL WELL MIXED. BAKE ON AN OILED GRIDDLE UNTIL NICELY BROWNED AND SERVE WITH HONEY, SYRUP OR JAM.

P.S. TO MAKE GREAT WAFFLES ADD 2 TBSP. OIL.

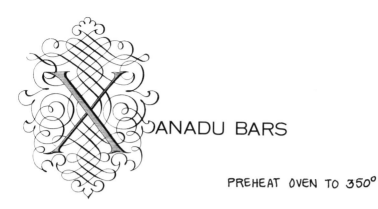

XANADU BARS

MELT 4 TBSP. BUTTER AND ADD 1/2 CUP BROWN SUGAR OR HONEY. STIR UNTIL DISSOLVED AND COOL. COMBINE THE FOLLOWING IN A FOOD PROCESSOR OR BLENDER:

1 TEASPOON VANILLA
1/4 TEASPOON SALT
1/3 CUP TOFU
1/2 CUP FLOUR
1 TEASPOON BAKING SODA
1 TEASPOON BAKING POWDER

MIX UNTIL UNTIL WELL BLENDED AND ADD THE BUTTER MIXTURE. STIR IN 1/2 CUP CHOPPED NUTS. IF YOU WANT TO VISIT XANADU, ADD SOME HERBS AS WELL.

BAKE AT 350° FOR 30 MINUTES. CUT INTO BARS. ENJOY.

35

Y AM OR PUMPKIN
MUFFINS

PREHEAT OVEN TO 425°

COMBINE THE FOLLOWING INGREDIENTS IN A BLENDER OR FOOD PROCESSOR AND BEAT UNTIL SMOOTH:

> 1/3 CUP TOFU
> 1/4 CUP OIL OR MELTED BUTTER
> 1/2 CUP BUTTERMILK
> 1/2 CUP YAM OR PUMPKIN
> 1/4 CUP SUGAR OR HONEY

IN A BOWL COMBINE THE DRY INGREDIENTS:

> 1/4 CUP UNPROCESSED BRAN
> 2 CUPS WHOLE WHEAT FLOUR
> 3 TEASPOONS BAKING POWDER
> 1/2 TEASPOON BAKING SODA
> 1/2 TEASPOON CINNAMON
> PINCH NUTMEG
> 1/4 TEASPOON SALT

POUR THE TOFU MIXTURE INTO THE FLOUR MIX AND <u>STIR</u> TOGETHER QUICKLY.
ADD 1/2 CUP CHOPPED NUTS AND 1/2 CUP RAISINS. THIS WILL MAKE ABOUT 24 2 INCH MUFFINS. BAKE AT 425° FOR ABOUT 20 MINUTES UNTIL CENTERS SPRING BACK WHEN PRESSED.

ZUCCHINI, STUFFED

PREHEAT OVEN TO 350°

SPLIT A 9 OR 10 INCH ZUCCHINI LENGTHWISE AND PARBOIL FOR ABOUT 10 MINUTES. DRAIN AND COOL. SCOOP OUT THE CENTERS OF THE HALVES AND SET ASIDE.

1/4 CUP CHOPPED ONIONS
1/4 CUP CHOPPED GREEN
   PEPPER
1 TBSP. OIL
2 TBSP. SUNFLOWER SEEDS
2 TBSP. CURRANTS OR
   RAISINS
3 TEASPOONS CURRY POWDER
SALT AND PEPPER TO TASTE

SAUTÉ THE VEGETABLES IN THE OIL UNTIL CLEAR. ADD THE SEEDS, RAISINS AND SPICES AND SAUTÉ FOR A FEW MINUTES, STIRRING ALL THE WHILE.

1 CUP TOFU
1 TBSP. FLOUR
MILK TO THIN, IF NECESSARY

MASH THE TOFU AND MIX IN THE FLOUR. ADD THE SAUTEED VEGETABLES AND MIX WELL. FILL THE TWO SQUASH HALVES AND PLACE IN A BAKING DISH.

CHOP THE INSIDES OF THE SQUASH AND COMBINE WITH OTHER COOKED VEGETABLES. ARRANGE IN DISH AND BAKE AT 350° FOR 30 MINUTES.

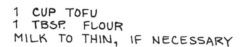

 ECIPES AND NOTES

On these two pages, dear Owner of This Book, perhaps Papa, Mamma, Brothers, Sisters, and others of your dear relations or friends will write their names and their recipes if you ask them to do so. Some day you may prize "The Tofu Primer" all the more for the sake of the writing held in these pretty settings of bloom and sunshine.

38

NDEX

IN